LIGHTNING
BOLT
BOOKS™

Inside the US Marine Corps

Jennifer Boothroyd

Lerner Publications • Minneapolis

For United States Marine Corps families

Lerner Publications Company
A division of Lerner Publishing Group, Inc.
241 First Avenue North
Minneapolis, MN 55401 USA

For reading levels and more information, look up this title at www.lernerbooks.com.

Library of Congress Cataloging-in-Publication Data

Names: Boothroyd, Jennifer, 1972- author.
Title: Inside the US Marine Corps / Jennifer Boothroyd.
Description: Minneapolis : Lerner Publications, [2017] | Series: Lightning bolt books. US Armed
    Forces | Includes bibliographical references and index. | Audience: Grades K-3.
Identifiers: LCCN 2016038207 (print) | LCCN 2016038343 (ebook) | ISBN 9781512433937
    (lb : alk. paper) | ISBN 9781512450682 (eb pdf)
Subjects: LCSH: United States. Marine Corps—Juvenile literature.
Classification: LCC VE23 .B59 2017 (print) | LCC VE23 (ebook) | DDC 359.9/60973—dc23

LC record available at https://lccn.loc.gov/2016038207

Manufactured in the United States of America
1-42029-23899-10/11/2016

Table of Contents

What is the US Marine Corps?

The US Marine Corps is a branch of the US military. Marines respond quickly to conflicts.

A conflict is a fight between two or more sides.

Marines often arrive by traveling through the water.

The Marine Corps is usually the first military branch to arrive when a conflict breaks out.

Many marines live on military bases, but some marines live on navy ships around the world. These marines can travel to conflicts even more quickly than others.

These marines are bringing supplies to people in need.

Marines aren't only called to fight. They also help rescue and protect people living in disaster areas.

Marine Corps Training

People must have special training to join the Marine Corps. It takes twelve weeks of training to master the skills needed to be a marine.

People training to be marines are called recruits.

Marines must be smart. Recruits spend many hours studying military history and strategy. They learn to be problem solvers.

Marines also need to be physically fit. Recruits learn hand-to-hand combat and how to use different weapons. They learn survival and first aid skills.

Combat is another word for fighting. These marines are practicing hand-to-hand combat.

Marines sometimes enter a fight by water. All their training prepares them for missions.

Recruits become strong swimmers. They learn to swim while carrying their heavy packs. Some learn water rescue skills.

All the recruits must pass a water test. They jump from an 8- to 10-foot (2.4- to 3-meter) platform into a pool and swim 82 feet (25 m) to the other end. They wear their uniforms and boots during the test.

After graduating from training, marines get more combat training. The Marine Corps is the only branch of the US military to give everyone this kind of extra training right after graduation.

Marine Corps Equipment

Marines use a lot of equipment. All marines are trained to use rifles, knives, and pistols. Marines wear gear that protects them and helps them fight.

Infantry marines fight on foot. They wear special vests for safety.

Many Marine Corps vehicles are amphibious. This means they can travel in water and on land. They have weapons and are built to protect the people inside.

Harrier jets are very useful. They can take off and land almost anywhere. The Super Stallion is the largest US military helicopter. It can carry people, supplies, and other vehicles.

This Harrier jet can take off by flying straight up.

The Marine Corps of the Future

The Marine Corps continues to develop new technology. Someday marines might use robots to carry heavy gear. The robots would be designed to follow marines.

The US Marine Corps might someday use robots like this one.

Exoskeleton suits help people carry very heavy equipment and gear. Marines would be able to walk farther and carry more with these special suits.

This is an exoskeleton suit.

The US Marine Corps is always prepared to keep our country safe.

Infantry Marine Gear Diagram

combat helmet

dust goggles

vest with pouches

combat blouse

combat gloves

combat trousers

combat boots

Marine Corps History

- The US Marine Corps was first created in 1775, but it was not made an official military branch until 1798.

- Women have served as marines since 1918 but could not fight in combat until recently. In 2016, all combat jobs became open to female marines.

- The LVT was the first amphibious vehicle used by the US Marine Corps. It was used during World War II (1939-1945).

Glossary

amphibious: able to work on land and in water

base: a place where members of the military live and work

combat: active fighting in a war

conflict: a struggle or fight

corps: a group of military members trained for special service

design: to make for a specific purpose

exoskeleton: a hard supporting or protective structure on the outside of the body

recruit: a person who is training to become a member of the US Marine Corps

technology: devices and tools that make finishing tasks easier or faster

Further Reading

Boothroyd, Jennifer. *How Do Helicopters Work?*
Minneapolis: Lerner Publications, 2013.

Jones, Keisha. *My Brother Is in the Marine Corps.*
New York: PowerKids, 2016.

Lüsted, Marcia Amidon. *Marine Force Recon: Elite Operations*. Minneapolis: Lerner Publications, 2014.

Marines: Equipment
http://www.marines.com/operating-forces/equipment

Murray, Julie. *United States Marine Corps.*
Minneapolis: Abdo Kids, 2015.

National Museum of the Marine Corps
http://www.usmcmuseum.com/making-marines.html

Index

Photo Acknowledgments

The images in this book are used with the permission of: Lance Cpl. Eryn Edelman/US Marines, pp. 2, 15; © Stocktrek Images, Inc./Alamy, p. 4; Sgt. Anthony Kirby/US Marines, p. 5; Seaman Craig Z. Rodarte/US Marines, p. 6; US Air Force photo/Staff Sgt. Marcus Morris, p. 7; Cpl. Walter D. Marino II/US Marines, pp. 8, 10; Sgt. Jose D. Lujano/US Marines, p. 9; Sgt. Benjamin E. Woodle/US Marines, p. 11; Marine Corps Photo by Lance Cpl. Caleb McDonald, p. 12; Sgt. Eric Keenan/US Marines, p. 13; US Marine Corps photo by Gunnery Sgt. Zachary Dyer, p. 14; Cpl. John Hamilton/US Marines, pp. 16, 23; Official USMC Photo by Kyle J. O. Olson, p. 17; © REX/Shutterstock, p. 18; Cpl. Aaron Patterson/US Marines, p. 19; Lance Cpl. Devan Gowans/US Marines, p. 20.

Front cover: Gunnery Sgt. Ismael Pena/U.S. Marines.

Main body text set in Billy Infant regular 28/36. Typeface provided by SparkType.